shack chic

PHOTOGRAPHY BY CRAIG FRASER

QUIVERTREE

PUBLICATIONS

CAPE TOWN, SOUTH AFRICA

PUBLISHED BY QUIVERTREE PUBLICATIONS, SOUTH AFRICA.

QUIVERTREE PUBLICATIONS
P O BOX 51051, WATERFRONT, 8002
CAPE TOWN, SOUTH AFRICA

TEL: +27 (0) 21 421 3355
FAX: +27 (0) 21 418 1671
E-MAIL: quivertree@doyle.co.za

ISBN NO: 0-620-28803-5

PHOTOGRAPHY © CRAIG FRASER 2002, DESIGN © DOYLE DESIGN® 2002.
PRINTED BY TIEN WAH PRESS, SINGAPORE. FIRST PRINTED IN 2002.
REPRODUCTION BY HIRT & CARTER CAPE (PTY) LTD

This book is dedicated to all shack dwellers
and their families,
especially those who welcomed us
into their homes.

We honour them and their achievements.

Enkosi.

A PERCENTAGE OF PROFITS FROM THIS BOOK WILL GO TO
UPLIFTMENT AND HOUSING FOR THE COMMUNITY.

'victory:
to build
a shack
and call it
home'

Sandile Dikeni

'hoUSeS are built on foundations with walls and roof. hOmes are built with things much deeper and less concrete'

Sandile Dikeni

architecture

'It's very important that even though a building may only be for temporary use,
it has to be pleasing to the eye – something of beauty.
A person has to be able to feel that this is home.'

SHIGERU BAN. JAPANESE ARCHITECT

The nature and sources of these building materials carry inherent limitations. As a result, structural deficiencies or architectural 'flaws' are inevitable.

But there is a system, believe it or not. One does not just arrive with a barrow-load of planks and start erecting a shack in any area. In the Western Cape, for instance, to be allowed to move into a particular neighbourhood, it is necessary to approach the community leaders in your prospective neighbourhood with a letter from the street committee in your previous area of residence vouching for your character. Criminal records and quarrelsome behaviour, for example, will diminish one's chances significantly.

No statistics could reveal the full truth of life as much as people themselves through the way they mediate their physical environments.

Shack Chic is an exhibition of cultural creativity in real life contexts.

Lining interior walls with branded 'wallpaper' - surplus packaging for popular South African products such as Lucky Star (pilchards), Bull Brand (corned beef), Lion matches, Sunlight soap, Colgate, Palmolive soap and Koo baked beans - is a popular décor scheme. Initially employed of necessity (functional for filling holes in the walls and covering the unsightly lack of uniformity in the building materials), they are more and more becoming a design feature in themselves. The effect of the step and repeat patterns of the paper is almost Warholian - terminally modern.

creativity

Many up-market décor shops in Cape Town and Johannesburg now offer a similar concept re-incarnated as screen-printed room partitions, lampshades, picture frames, lunch boxes and other items. The shack dwellers' inventiveness has spawned a trend that is probably the closest Sandton will ever get to Soweto in terms of aesthetic concord.

The migration from rural to urban areas has added interesting and imaginative interpretations to the creative process and transformed these mere physical dwelling places, as humble as they seem, into spiritual abodes. There is no fear of contradiction in the rural-meets-urban aesthetic that simultaneously and unapologetically juxtaposes cow horns sourced from ritual slaughter in honour of ancestors, hanging above the doorpost against Madonna-and-child icons reverently covered in protective clear plastic paper hanging on the 'living room' wall.

Photographs of loved ones are cherished in the overall scheme of décor. Usually taken by a local photographer who does the rounds daily, taking photographs of members of the community and returning on an appointed day to deliver the developed product, these cost R4 each (the average price of a loaf of bread).

commUNity

The literal meaning of 'umuntu ngumuntu nga bantu' is 'a person is a person because of other people'. In other words, you are who you are because of others. Expressed variously as 'Botho' in Sotho and Tswana, and 'Ubuntu' in the Nguni languages, this concept is about a strong sense of community where people co-exist in a mutually supportive lifestyle.

Neighbours avail themselves to mind your children while you are out looking for work. They will call in a personal favour or incur a debt on your behalf by organising a lift with someone they barely know through a 'cousin' to take your ill grandmother/spouse/child to hospital. They will take up a monetary offering in the neighbourhood or at their job in the city to help you pay your bus fare to the funeral of a distant uncle. They will even attend the funeral of someone in the area, no matter how little they knew them, as a show of support to the deceased's family.

(Someone involved in this project took an entire day off to cook and assist at the funeral of a man she had never met in her life but whom she heard came from her parents' village in the Transkei, nearly a full day's drive away. She herself was born and raised in the township and had visited Transkei only a few times in her life. Her rationale: "That's not a good way to die. I would hate to die in a place where no one knew me and no one came to my funeral.")

The larger the gathering at your passing, the greater significance your life gains. (Esther Zulu, Librarian, Mayibuye Centre). People are confident enough to migrate from the rural area of their origin on the strength of knowing someone from that area now living in the city. On arrival, they can expect to be hosted *gratis* until they find a job and place of their own. Irrespective of blood ties, significant as those are in African terms, in this peri-urban context, for purposes of maintaining social order, security, communion, financial and moral support, you 'choose' people as your family and they choose you.

In the end, this is the most prized feature of life in the informal settlement.

'umuntu ngumuntu 'nga bantu'

Ancient African maxim

line

order

colOur

go

'Home, it's where your great people are, where you get blessings,
where the graves of your grandparents are.'
NOMA AFRICA SWELINDAWO

'it is
love
in the home that
builds it,
and that is what makes us
happy'

MCITWA NDABA, NO.83, SPECIAL QUARTER, LANGA

Life is a blank canvas inviting self expression. The choice and juxtaposition of colour creates vibrant energy.

colOur

Unconventional use of colour defines Shack Chic. It is unpredictable and diverse. It follows no rules. It is both accidental and deliberate. It is constrained by resource limitations but always strikingly unique.

No two shacks are identical.

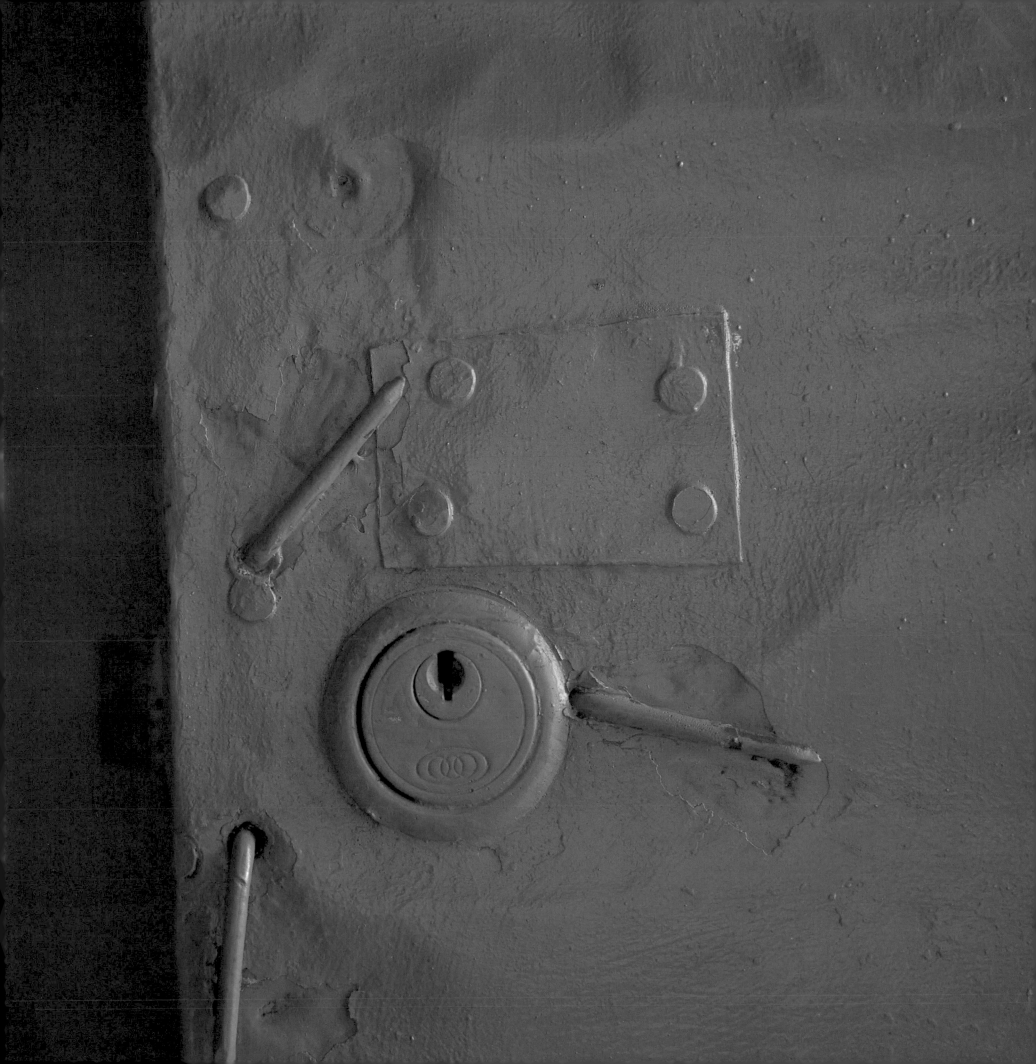

'I live pleasurably
here
for we have a
motto of treating
each other
juStly'

LAWRENCE SIKHUNDLA - BLOCK 8, NO.166, PHILIPPI

'I love

Bob Marley most when he sings *One Love* and Jahman's song entitled *Two Sides of Love*, because I believe it's nothing but love that will

set us free

from hate and jealousy'

LAWRENCE SIKHUNDLA · BLOCK 8, NO.166, PHILIPPI

'Home is where I was born, it's where my umbilical cord is.'
PHEKO MONATSI, 3571 HEMPE STR

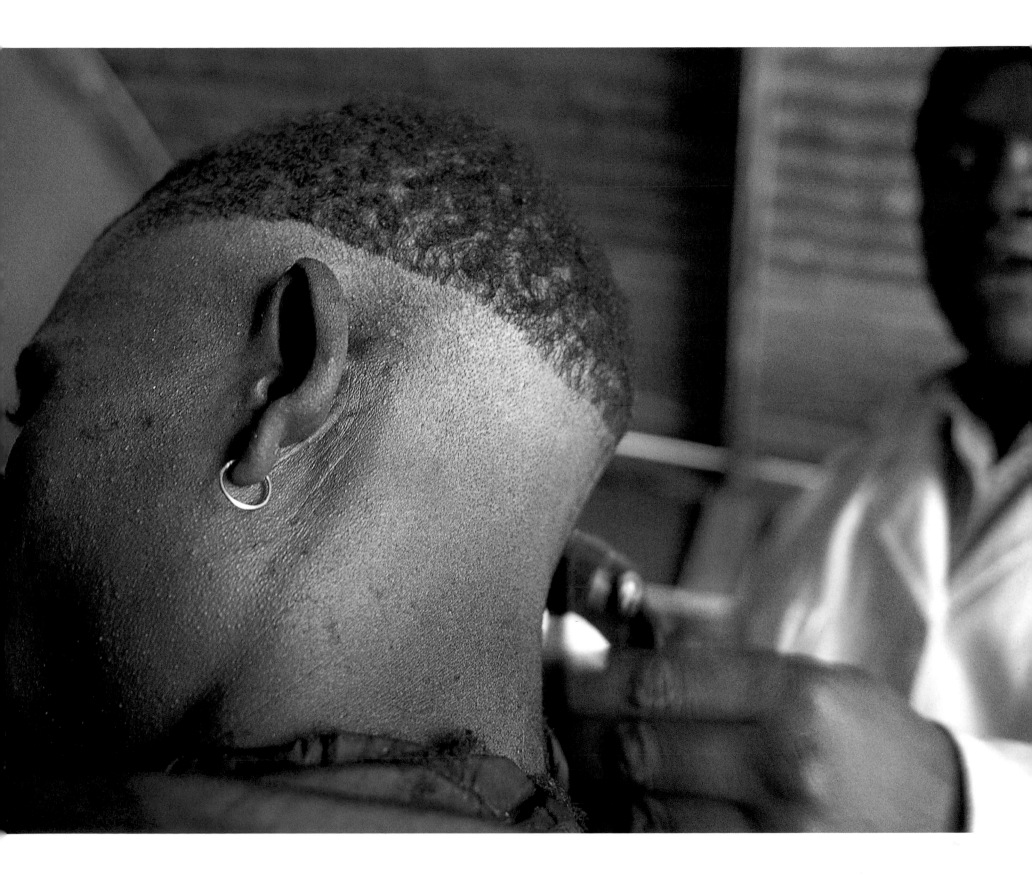

'my artistIC personality is reflected most in my home. you can see piCtures on the wall, a collage that I am busy with and my in-house workshop says a lot about my personality and my inclination if not my destiny in life'

THEMBA MAJEBE, A31, BROWN'S FARM, PHILIPPI

'There is no money that can buy that picture, it symbolises my respect and my humble honour to mother nature.'
ELLIOT XOLANI MRHWETYANA, BROWN'S FARM, PHILIPPI

LEBOMBO
PIESANGS

LEBOMBO
BANANAS

ENKEL   14°C   SINGLE

'A home means so much and everything to me - it's where my spirit resides, it's where I communicate with my ancestors in their visits at night in my dreams.'

LAWRENCE SIKHUNDLA - BLOCK 8, No.166, PHILIPPI

'I hate **private** life ... I grew up at a **home** where everyone at every time was **welcomed**'

GEORGE BANJWA, DIRECTOR OF SENTINAL FOODS, MANDELA PARK

'We live as if we were born by the same parents. They will pick me up when I am down, they will clothe me when I am naked and they will definitely feed me when I am hungry.'

THEMBA MAJEBE, A31, BROWN'S FARM, PHILIPPI

'If there is an overproduction of fish I don't wait for it to get rotten. I bring it here and
give it to people while it's still fresh, for free.'

GEORGE BANJWA, DIRECTOR OF SENTINAL FOODS, MANDELA PARK

'there is something sensual about the rattle of rain on a corrugated roof'

Sandile Dikeni

'Texture: the character, appearance or consistency of a surface or a textile fabric as determined by the arrangement and thickness of its threads.'

Based on the above dictionary definition, Shack Chic is about texture in huge amounts. The surfaces are a multimedia patchwork of wood grain, plastic, cardboard, sand, zinc, vinyl, concrete, brick, cotton, satin, sisal, paper, mud, fine dust, chicken feathers, crocheted bedspreads, wool, curly hair ...

texture

In this eclectic mix of textures, Shack Chic expressively mirrors the reality of life - shiny and dull in patches, hard and soft in places, tough and fragile in turn.

The discarded rudiments of other people's pasts are reincarnated into vibrant and living elements of the present. In a society where practically everything is obtained second or third hand, found objects are shaken free of their previous associations to take on a whole new and permanent part in the life of the home.

'I believe that if you are

clean,

chances are
your

heart

is also clean'

LAWRENCE SIKHUNDLA · BLOCK 8, NO.166, PHILIPPI

'We are five. The three children are not mine, they were left by their mother who passed away.'
NOMA AFRIKA, SOLIDANE MAKHAZA, 36022, MBEKO STR.

light

Sunlight, candlelight, lamplight, torchlight, electric light ... Whatever form it comes in, light is coveted by the human species for more than the mere purpose of dispelling darkness.

It is the one element that is able to create mood and lend magic even to the most humble space. It creates a natural flow between interior and exterior and has a supernatural energy that promotes a sense of spaciousness even in the most cramped dwelling.

Shack Chic is the delightful lustre of light as it falls on the reflective surfaces of highly polished furniture, zinc wash buckets and a thousand foil wrappers. It is the ambience, dream-like in quality, that illuminates objects, elevating them from their mundane status to an almost fantastical surreal transparency.

'I do the paintings by using coloured papers.'
NTOMBENKOSI MRADU, 51, BROWN'S FARM, PHILIPPI

'I miss the stars and that darkness and also to see those women with clay on their faces.'
NTOMBENKOSI MRADU, 51, BROWN'S FARM, PHILIPPI

SANDILE DIKENI (POET)

Sandile Dikeni, a poet and columnist, is the author of two collections of poetry, *Guava Juice* (Mayibuye Books 1992) and *Telegraph to the Sky* (University of Natal Press 2000). His work has also been anthologised in many journals and collaborations including Staffrider (SA), New Observations (New York), Wasafiri (London), Khayelitsha: 14-2-95, a collaboration with Alesandro Esteri (Italy). He has been translated into French, Hebrew and Italian.

His collection of columns and articles, *Soul Fire* (University of Natal Press 2000), has just been released. He currently lives in Pretoria.

ABLE MPUTING (JOURNALIST)

Before enrolling at UCT he studied creative writing. In 1992 he obtained a Diploma in Jazz Theory and obtained a third grade in classical theory with distinction. After finishing his music diploma, he became a co-founder of The Jam band and recorded a song on a CD compilation with the New World Music company.

During the course of his degree at UCT he also studied film, English and literature, and joined the Afro African Film Resource Organisation. In 1998, he accepted a post as an Assistant Cultural Officer at the Centre for African Studies at UCT.

He now works as a freelance writer and contributes to publications such as *The Cape Times, Tribute Magazine, Sunday World, Big Issue* and *Cape Argus*.

MLUNGISI GEGANA (OUR GUIDE AND TRANSLATOR)

Mlungisi grew up in a farming town in the Eastern Cape. He started playing music when he was 12 years old using a three string guitar which he had made from nylon and a five litre tin.

In 1986 Mlungisi went to Cape Town to further his musical career. He met bassist, Godfrey Ntsila, and took the bass up as his preferred instrument. Self-taught, he played for various local bands.

Subsequently, Mlungisi studied a few years of music at MAPP School of Music at the University of Cape Town but was forced to give up due to lack of funds. He is now a freelance bass player, living in Johannesburg.